COMFORT
from
HEAVEN

COMFORT
from
HEAVEN

*The peace of God directly from
Heaven to heal your broken Heart*

JOHN H DUNBAR

XULON PRESS

Xulon Press
2301 Lucien Way #415
Maitland, FL 32751
407.339.4217
www.xulonpress.com

Unless otherwise indicated, Scripture quotations taken from the Holy Bible, New International Version (NIV). Copyright © 1973, 1978, 1984, 2011 by Biblica, Inc.™. Used by permission. All rights reserved.

Paperback ISBN-13: 978-1-66283-431-8
Ebook ISBN-13: 978-1-66283-432-5

Dedication

Whenever I had an opportunity to introduce Bert, I often did so in this manner: I would like to introduce you to the most influential person in my life, my friend, a trusted counselor, a person who has brought an eternal value to my life. The fact that she is my wife, well I try very hard not to take her for granted. This is Roberta, or Bert as I call her. This book is dedicated to her in appreciation of her love for her family. Personally, her love for me and patience with me "has raised me up to be more that I could ever have been on my own". In this, there is no doubt or discussion.

THE BOOK

This book started out as a journal of Bert's hospital stay and text messages to family and friends. It has turned into a journal of the ***Comfort from Heaven*** given to us. The spiritual experiences are from family and friends. They are documented as best I could, as soon after they occurred. The intention of this book is to encourage the reader to believe they can have similar experiences. Seeing, hearing, perceiving and receiving ***Comfort from Heaven***. Seek the Lord, Jesus Christ, and what His sacrifice means to you personally and He will be found.

JUST FOR YOU

You, the reader, just as you are! No need to consider your past actions or beliefs. No need to join an organization. There are no right words to say. The condition of your heart is all that matters. Consider this: the Savior willingly laid down His life for you. He paid a ransom for you that you could not pay. None of us will ever or could ever do anything worthy of this sacrifice. His love for you, for all of us has been demonstrated for all time. We have been created to walk with Him, feel His presence, hear His voice, and see His hand in our own personal journey!

Jerimiah 29:13 (NIV)
You will seek, strive after meet and acquire me
When you seek and strive after me with your whole heart;
which are your feelings, your will and even your intellect

To say it one more time: you do not have to be anything other than who you are today. Hearing, seeing, and perceiving God's hand in your life is something that you can experience. This is based on the belief and the experiences shared in this book that God is always communicating to His children. His Love is paramount and by definition means, "more important than anything else". Do you, the reader, understand that His love for you is paramount? You are worthy of that love!

TABLE OF CONTENTS

Listed by Comforts, Received by Date

Monday, February 15, 2021 (First *Comfort*):
Prior to anyone getting sick. Comfort in preparation 1

Monday, February 22, 2021 (Second *Comfort*):
Granddaughter's dream. Comfort in preparation 6

Tuesday, February 23, 2021 (Third *Comfort*):
Granddaughter's dream. Comfort in preparation 7

Wednesday, February 24, 2021 (Fourth *Comfort*):
Grandson's dream. Comfort in preparation. 8

Saturday, February 27, 2021 (Fifth *Comfort*):
Good-bye for now. Comfort in preparation. 11

Saturday, March 6, 2021 – Friday, March 19, 2021:
What we believe and how we acted as a family 18

Thursday, March 18, 2021 (Sixth *Comfort*):
Megan and the five birds. Comfort in preparation 23

Friday, March 19, 2021: 11:00 p.m. CST.
The day that Bert went home to be with The Lord 25

Saturday, March 20, 2021 (Seventh *Comfort*):
Awakened by a song. ***Comfort from Heaven.*** 32

Saturday, March 20, 2021 (Eighth Comfort):
Walking with Jesus. ***Comfort from Heaven*** 34

Saturday, March 20, 2021 (Ninth *Comfort*):
Daughter sensing & feeling Mom's presence.
Comfort from Heaven. . . . . , , ,   , , ,   , , ... , , , 36

Sunday, March 21, 2021 (Tenth *Comfort*):
Daughter called by a very special nick-name.
Comfort from Heaven. 37

Wednesday, March 24, 2021 (Eleventh *Comfort*):
Grief changed from heartache to simply sadness.
Comfort from Heaven. 38

Wednesday, March 24, 2021 (Twelfth *Comfort*):
Granddaughter sharing the good news.
Comfort from Heaven. 40

Thursday, March 25, 2021 (Thirteenth *Comfort*):
Daughter receiving a personal message delivered
in a humorous and personal way. ***Comfort from Heaven*** 41

Saturday, March 27, 2021 (Fourteenth Comfort):
Granddaughter sharing with her mom.
Comfort from Heaven. 43

Tuesday, March 30, 2021 (Fifteenth *Comfort*):
Granddaughter sharing with her mom.
Comfort from Heaven. 44

Tuesday, March 30, 2021 (Sixteenth *Comfort*):
Daughter's dream validating her mom is still
a part of our lives. ***Comfort from Heaven*** 45

Friday, April 2, 2021 (Seventeenth *Comfort*):
Daughter's dream concerning a miscarriage.
Comfort from Heaven 47

Friday, April 2, 2021 (Eighteenth *Comfort*):
Husband receiving peace deep within on
upcoming anniversary.
Comfort from Heaven 48

Thursday, April 15, 2021 (Nineteenth *Comfort*):
Who is this? ***Comfort from Heaven*** 51

Wednesday, April 21, 2021 (Twentieth):
Daughter sensing that her mom's earthly
hurts & disappointments are now healed in heaven.
Comfort from Heaven 53

Thursday, May 20, 2021 (Twenty-first *Comfort*):
The twin daughters across the country from each other.
Are together in feelings and emotions.
Comfort from Heaven 54

Thursday, May 27, 2021 (Twenty-second *Comfort*):
Daughters heart desire met. ***Comfort from Heaven*** 56

Tuesday, June 22, 2021 (Twenty-third *Comfort*):
Rejoicing with us. ***Comfort from Heaven*** 58

PROLOGUE

Our Family
John Hugh Dunbar - Born: February 28, 1952
Roberta (Bert) Marie Wallace- Born: November 1, 1952
John & Bert - Married: April 23, 1973
Coleen - Born: January 24, 1974
Kelly - Born: April 16, 1976
Joshua - Born: January 9, 1984
Megan and Molly - Born: November 28, 1986

Note to the readers, I will always speak of Bert, in the present tense. I will never consciously speak of her in the past tense. As I am forever changed as a person for having known her and her influence continues today.

Thoughts on Reading this Book:

The book is written in a way that allows you, the reader, to select from the table of contents what you might want to read. If you think your grief is too new and great, and you do not want to read about another person's passing, then do not. Pick out a *Comfort from Heaven* that sparks interest in you. Something that you can relate to: a dream, a song, something from God's creation, anything.

Background:

I have been blessed by the one and only Almighty God, the Creator of the Universe, to have been raised by my mom, Mary Klein Dunbar and married to Roberta "Bert" Wallace Dunbar. Under my mom's guidance, I understood what commitment is, how to have and live by faith in the darkest of situations. Additionally, based on my mom's steadfastness in her convictions, I received a solid Catholic education until the eighth grade. I will always acknowledge that this is the foundation of my faith. My counselor, Bert, built on this and guided me to establish a very personal, unwavering relationship with my Savior, the Christ, Jesus of Nazareth. Both of these strong independent, godly women stayed with me, never gave up on me and taught me by example.

Acts 2:17-18 (NIV)

2:17) In the last, the final, end of days,

God, the Supreme Divinity says,

I will pour, spill out my Spirit, the Holy Spirit,

the Spirit Mind on all people.

Your sons and daughters will prophesy, foretell

events and speak under inspiration.

Your young men less than 40 years old, will see visions, an inspired

appearance capable of being seen; your old men will dream,

dreams, having visions while sleeping.

2:18) Even on my servants under bondage, both men and women.

I will pour, spill out my Spirit, the Holy Spirit, the Spirit Mind in

those days, and they will prophesy, foretell events

and speak under inspiration'

Monday, February 15, 2021
(First *Comfort from Heaven*)

Bert and Kelly's discussion

We had been experiencing a heavy snowstorm and most everything was closed. What Bert and I always liked to do was, when we have a storm like this, we would get in our car and drive around and enjoy the beauty of the snow (and the few cars on the road). While we were out, we decided to go over to Kelly and Rob's house to visit. As always, we have a very nice visit with Kelly, Rob (saw him briefly as he was working in his office), Johnny, and Brooke. When we were getting ready to leave, Kelly was sitting next to Bert on the sofa and Bert said, "I never want to leave this place". Kelly did not answer, but thought what her mom shared was very different, as she never talked like this.

This was the first *Comfort from Heaven*, but we did not recognize it as preparation.

Tuesday, February 16, 2021

Rob (Kelly's husband) is getting sick, very quickly getting sicker.

Wednesday, February 17, 2021

Bert getting sick

Bert was feeling terrible, but thinking it was just some flu-like symptoms.

Thursday, February 18, 2021

Rob (Kelly's husband) is very sick and at the hospital. Tested positive for COVID.

Because of this, Bert agrees to be tested for COVID.

Friday, February 19, 2021

Bert getting sicker

Bert's test results are positive for COVID. She is becoming very sick and weak, and agrees to go to the hospital in an ambulance. Bert is in the ER from 4:30 p.m. until after midnight. Receives some fluids and antibiotics. The ER was full and this was not a good experience. I brought Bert home about 1:00 a.m.

Monday, February 22, 2021
(Second *Comfort from Heaven*)

Brooke's (Kelly's daughter) dream

Brooke had a dream in which she was playing and was inside a short wall that was blocking her from getting to her Gram. Brooke could see Gram over the wall, but she could not get to her. Brooke tried kicking the wall down to get to gram, but could not knock it down.

The second *Comfort from Heaven*, but we did not recognize it as preparation.

Tuesday, February 23, 2021
(Third *Comfort from Heaven*)

Natalie's (Megan's daughter) dream

Natalie (Meagan and Justin's four-year-old daughter) had a dream that she was visiting gram, who was in her bed. In addition, Brooke came in to visit with her.

The third *Comfort from Heaven*, but we did not recognize it as preparation.

Wednesday, February 24, 2021
(Fourth *Comfort from Heaven*)

Johnny's (Kelly's son) dream

Johnny (Kelly and Rob's eight-year-old son) had a dream that we were in the backyard and having a fire in our fireplace (we would have fires from time to time and roast marshmallows). Johnny noticed something unusual about gram. He then said to the gram in the dream, "You are not my real Grammy."

The fourth *Comfort from Heaven*, but we did not recognize it as preparation.

Thursday, February 25, 2021

Discussed with Bert's doctor the oxygen saturation level if it drops to 82 percent, she must go to the hospital. Normal for a healthy person is 96 to 98 percent.

Friday, February 26, 2021

Bert had a terrible night. Coughing all night, but no fever. Bert's oxygen saturation was between 81 and 87 percent, staying at 81 percent at the time of the call to the doctor at 8:00 a.m.

The doctor explained to Bert how serious this was and that she needed to go to the hospital immediately. Bert was reluctant due to her recent experience, which she told her doctor about. Bert was very clear that going to the ER was no help and that she was not treated seriously or with respect. Bert shared that she did not intend to go to the ER again.

The doctor changed her tone of voice and actually said, "Roberta, you will pass in your bed." She also said that she would have a team waiting for her when she arrived at the hospital, and that we could go to a different hospital within the system. Bert growled reluctantly and agreed to go.

An aside: Whenever Bert realized she had lost a discussion or was not going to get her way, she would "growl" in agreement. The translation of the growl is, "OK, but don't push it."

This was the second time Bert was picked up by the ambulance service and the fire fighters and ambulance team members were respectful, kind, and very efficient. When Bert arrived at the ER, there was a team waiting for her and they started to help her immediately. Bert was placed in the COVID ward and began a ten-day quarantine. Beginning with today, I would check in with Bert's nurses twice a day; once mid-morning and then early evening.

Saturday, February 27, 2021
(Fifth *Comfort from Heaven*)

The "good-bye for now" text, 1:00 p.m.
Bert was admitted the day before. She rebounded from a very bad condition that day. Bert was taken to the hospital by ambulance on Friday, February 26. On Saturday, at about 1:00 p.m. in the afternoon, after exchanging text messages, it was apparent that Bert was considering being put on a ventilator and to be unconscious for two and a half weeks. She then sent me the following text:

"I am so sorry I was so miserable and difficult. Some of it was the no air, I guess, and some of it just rotten me. Thanks for your present, patient love and care. You can always be counted on, and are the dearest gift of God to me. My greatest support and I love you with all my heart. If I get a second chance, I will do better. Please tell all the kids what treasures they are. Johnny must keep seeking God and Josh must seek God for His truth. They all must keep coming to know God more and more all the time. I love you forever, my best friend and handsome husband."

When I read the message, I asked myself, "What is she saying? Is Bert saying good-bye?" I was very emotional the rest of the day. I struggled throughout the day just to do small things. I did not want to face the fact that Bert knew she was going home to be with the Lord, and that she was preparing me for it.

The fifth ***Comfort from Heaven***, but I did not want to recognize it as preparation.

Sunday, February 28, 2021

Bert had a positive day in which her oxygen saturation number was in the mid-nineties. The pulmonologist shared that if Bert kept this up, she would not need a ventilator. Bert was very pleased, and we were thanking God for answering our prayers. Bert did not forget to wish me a Happy Birthday!

Monday, March 1, 2021

Bert had a very bad day and all day long her breaths per minute were high in the mid- to upper thirties. Normal breaths per minute is twenty. Breathing like this puts a tremendous strain on the heart.

Tuesday, March 2, 2021

Bert's day was worse than yesterday.

At 10:26 a.m. on Tuesday, Bert's pulmonologist left me a message and asked that I return the call immediately. I called back and we talked. The doctor explained that Bert's heart rate was very high due to her trying to breath and that her breaths per minute were forty-five to fifty and that heart failure was a serious concern. She explained that she was respecting Bert's stated wishes not to be put on a ventilator, but she just wanted to make sure that this is what she wanted, because Bert was, in effect, dying. She shared that they could give her morphine, but that would not prevent her from dying.

"Bert is in quarantine, but can I come and in and talk to her?" I asked.

The doctor said, "Absolutely," and she let me know how to get to Bert.

When I arrived at the hospital, I was allowed to go right up to the fourth floor and to the nurse's station. I met the receptionist and Bert's nurse. These were some of the people I had been talking to over the last couple of days. I put on a gown and gloves and the nurse went in with me to see Bert. I sat down beside her and just held her hand in mine.

"I love you," I said. "All the kids, everyone sends their love."

Even with the oxygen mask on Bert was breathing very quickly: thirty to thirty-five breaths per minute. She could hardly say a word

14

without losing breath. She was trying to talk, but I could not understand her and the nurse could not either.

Bert took the mask off with the help of her nurse and said, "I can't keep this up much longer." She meant trying to breathe.

I was sitting beside her with her hand in mine. I said, "That is why I am here. Bert, you are not doing good. You are slipping away. I want to talk with you about your decision not to be put on a ventilator."

"If I am slipping, how will that help me to come back?" Bert asked.

Bert's nurse shared that being on a ventilator will give her lungs time to heal and give her a much-needed rest.

Bert looked me straight in my eyes. "So then, I'm dying."

"Yes," I said, looking her straight in her eyes.

"So, I will never see you again?" Bert asked.

"Not this side of Heaven, but we will be together again," I said. "I don't want you to go, we all want you to stay and not go. Bert, I want you to take this chance that it will help you get better."

Bert was quiet and closed her eyes for a few minutes, trying to breathe. She then opened her eyes and, extending her hands, palms up, she said reluctantly, "What choice do I have?" She closed her eyes again. She was so tired.

I waited for a few minutes before speaking again, waited because I knew the fighter that Bert was and I did not want to push it. After a few short minutes, I asked, "Bert, are you willing to be put on a ventilator?"

Bert nodded her head, "Yes".

Bert's nurse smiled at me and said, "I will call the doctor right now."

Bert was so tired that she was going in and out of consciousness.

Just sitting there with Bert, for the next fifteen minutes or so, I was thinking so many different thoughts.

After almost fifty years of knowing Bert, this was too short a time. How many things that I would like to have done differently.

15

How very strange this is. I am holding the hand of my dying wife and I have the same disease, but have no symptoms!

Just sitting, looking at the most influential person in my life I have ever known.

Still believing that God will answer our prayers and allow her to stay!

The team of nurses came in. I met Bert's doctor, and she thanked me for coming in and talking to mom. She seemed relieved. As I waited outside the room, the team completed their task of putting Bert on the ventilator.

The receptionist came and got me. I was allowed to go in to say good-bye "for now".

Going in, I saw what was explained to me, what I would see. Bert had both arms restrained so that, if she was startled, she would not pull out any of the tubing. Bert was fast asleep. I put my hand on her hand.

"I love you more than my own life itself," I said. "You are the best thing that has ever happened to me and this family. Thank you for agreeing to do this for me. Looking forward to seeing you soon."

I looked at Bert for a few minutes and then left her in God's hands. Multiple times over the course of the next two weeks, I would share with family and friends that I left her in God's hands, and I was not taking her back. This meant that I was ready to accept whatever God had for us as a family.

When I left, Bert's breaths per minute were at twenty-five and she was keeping pace with the ventilator. This was a very good sign. From this point, I would send out text messages to family and friends two times a day to update them on Bert's condition.

Wednesday, March 3, 2021 -
Friday, March 5, 2021

We were looking forward to Saturday when the quarantine was to be lifted and we could visit with Bert.

Twice a day, I talked to the nurses on duty. Bert was holding her own with breaths per minute at 25-26 and oxygen saturation levels low 90's. In addition, her x-rays showed no progression of the pneumonia Bert had from the onset of COVID.

Saturday, March 6, 2021 – Friday, March 19, 2021

We (our family) believe that we are created in our God's (Father, Son, and Spirit) image (body, soul, and spirit). Whenever possible, my mom's side of our family would practice what they called "a vigil", taking turns spending time with a family member who was gravely ill so that someone was with them until the end of their life.

As a young person, I have personally gone with my mom to visit gravely ill family members at the hospital. I have been with Bert when she sat with individuals in an unconscious state and Bert would speak to their spirit. She would pray for them, tell those stories that make you laugh, remember wonderful memories, and share appreciation for all the individual had done.

This is what we believe and this what we do, another example of how my mom and Bert have influenced me and now our family.

Therefore, when we (Kelly, Megan, Josh, and I) visited with Bert, we not only told stories, but kept her updated on the family and also shared messages from her brothers and sisters, love, prayers.

From her sister Helen who lives in Pennsylvania: "Hey, Bert. Get up and paint something, will ya?!" You have to know the relationship they have and Helen's sense of humor. This message made us all laugh!

Bert was famous within the family for creating beautiful pieces of art from the most unlikely objects. Josh and I were the first to visit with Bert. The girls wanted us to go first and then we could prepare them to visit Bert. She was sedated to the point of being unconscious, but her arms were not restrained. It was not as bad as I thought it was going to be, but then again, I was desperate to see her, so it would not have mattered what she looked like.

Having Josh there with me proved a tremendous support for me through this. He was steady as a rock through everything.

The girls (Kelly and Megan) came and we visited every day.

The hospital staff in the COVID ward were gracious to us in every way. No questions were left unanswered, no matter how many times we asked the same or similar questions.

Wednesday, March 17, 2021

Afternoon

Josh, Kelly, and I were visiting and all seemed as good as it had been for days. Suddenly, Bert's heart rate rose rapidly. Josh and I both were schooled in how to read all the monitors and we understood the severity of the situation.

We stood back and watched the team of nurses respond (Bert's doctors were in the hospital and online watching and directing the team). Bert was crashing right before our eyes.

Kelly looked into my eyes to gauge my reaction, then she turned to her brother. He reached out and held her close whispering, "It will be alright. It will be alright." I have never been prouder of our son. When it counted the most, he offered his strength to his sister.

After what seemed to be about thirty minutes, Bert was stable. The nurse came in, handed me the phone, and said, "The doctor wants to talk to you."

The doctor explained he was involved in every step of what had just transpired. He then shared that he lost his father to COVID two weeks prior. "Mr. Dunbar, with Roberta's condition at this time, I do not see a path to recovery."

I thought about what I just heard and asked, "So then, doctor, is it time to call the family?"

"I cannot predict how Roberta will do from here, but I would call family," he said.

I ended the call with a "thank you, sir," and turned to Kelly and Josh and said that I was going to the waiting room to make phone calls to Megan, Molly, and Coleen, and to Bert's family. They left the room and came with me.

I called Coleen first and then Molly to let them know how grave the situation was. Helen, Bert's sister, was the person I was using as a point person to communicate to Bert's family. I shared with Helen, cried with her, and apologized that I was asking her to share with the family. She said that it was OK and I committed to let her know of any changes.

I did not share with anyone, at this time, what the doctor had said about not seeing a path to recovery for Bert. I decided I would carry this opinion/burden alone.

Wednesday, March 17, 2021 – Thursday, March 18, 2021 (Sixth *Comfort from Heaven*)

Late Afternoon – Early Evening

Megan and her family had rented a cabin at Lake Keystone (twenty-five minutes from the hospital) well in advance of this day. Megan's husband, Justin, and the children, Natalie and Rudy, absolutely loved being outdoors and spending time at the lake. I had been I contact with Meagan and, at this time, she knew that Bert was rebounding from earlier in the day and her condition looked promising.

From Megan: "I was at Lake Keystone on spring break with Justin and the kids. Of course, this week was very hard and I was constantly praying for Mom and asking God to please show me He was with us in this situation. One thing I saw when praying with Molly over the phone were five birds that kept flying to the branches in front of me. They would fly away, then all come back and look at me. It was strange enough that I counted the birds; each time there were five. Looking back, that could have been a symbol of us all being together; the five children all together when mom passed and how we wouldn't have been able to get through it without each other. Mom also knew that she could go home to Heaven because we were together."

Megan and her family were back home Friday morning.

The sixth *Comfort from Heaven* and Megan was considering the possible interpretations, but at the same time, not wanting to recognize it as preparation.

Thursday, March 18, 2021

The doctor was in when Josh and I were visiting Bert. We talked about Bert's condition and that the next day, Friday, she was going to be moved to a non-COVID intensive care ward within the hospital as her additional days of quarantine were completed.

The doctor and I were talking about our desire to have what is called a "Full Code", meaning that if a person's heart stops, the team of doctors and nurses will do everything to revive the patient. The doctor said that, over the last year, the hospital has had only one COVID patient who walked out of the hospital after having received a "Full Code". Josh was standing close by and I had a sense that he was listening. I told the doctor that we wanted a "Full Code" response if that situation was to happen.

We finished our discussion and then I turned to Josh and explained that I shared with the doctor that if the situation with Bert changed for the worse, I needed to be contacted immediately and that we wanted a "Full Code" response. I ended this conversation by telling Josh, "We will do everything we can for mom, as that is what she would do for us."

Josh said he agreed and understood.

I did not realize how this decision would play such a major part the next evening and our lives moving forward. No matter what was going to happen, I needed to be with Bert when it happened so that she knew that she was not alone. No matter how unthinkable Bert's passing would be, much worse for me was the thought that I would not be with her at the end of her life. I made it clear to the doctors and nurses multiple times: I have to be here with her. Again, the team on the COVID floor were always gracious to us.

I heard back from Coleen and Molly and they had made reservations to arrive tomorrow morning.

Friday, March 19, 2021

There is a special person in my life who is always there to listen and understand. Never giving advice or an opinion, but always to pray for me and mine. In many areas of our spiritual walk, our beliefs are similar if not the same.

Since the events of Wednesday, when Bert took a turn for the worse and Collen and Molly had made preparations to be here in Tulsa today (Molly from New York at 11:00 a.m. and Coleen from Pennsylvania at noon), I had a thought; a nagging discomfort deep within my spirit. I had to talk to someone, but the thought I had was not one I would/could share with the children. I needed a special someone to share this with, to unload.

Molly had arrived at concourse A and Josh and I greeted her. After some time together, we walked over to concourse B to greet Coleen. At this time, I shared that I needed to make a phone call and went to be by myself to call that someone.

JW is that someone. I called him and, as always, he answered.

"JW, I have a nagging thought that is eating me up and I need to share it with someone, and you are that someone," I said.

"Go ahead," he said.

"The thought I have is this: all of our children will be here together today, and we are coming together as a family for the first time in 5 plus years. Could it be that Bert is hanging on, fighting to stay here with us until we are all together?"

He said, "Yes, I believe that is what could be happening, knowing how much Bert loved all her children and how she always wanted them to be close."

JW and his lovely wife, Vicki, have always been close to Bert and I. Bert's love of her family (children, grandchildren, sisters, and brothers) was always forefront and, if you understood that, you understood Bert. This is what Bert has always been about: family.

We talked some more, and I explained that Molly was in and we were waiting for Coleen. As always, as I was ending my conversation with JW, I was in a different place, a better place after talking with him. The thought was not affecting me like before, but I did not want to embrace the thought as if it were true and going to happen.

It was time for Coleen to arrive and, when I saw her coming down the hallway from her gate, I realized that there were others walking by her, but I was totally focused on our first-born Coleen. As I walked up to her, I noticed someone walking close to her and my thought was that if they did not move out of my way, then I would move them. However, I did not even look at them: my eyes were on Coleen only.

We embraced, hugged, kissed, and cried. Then I let her be greeted by her brother, Josh, and her sister, Molly.

As I released her from my arms, she asked, "Do you see who is with me?"

I then turned and looked at the person who was walking so close to her. It was my younger brother, Jim (who I also had not seen in five years).

I greeted him with, "What the hell are you doing here?"

"Where else would I be?" He responded.

I grabbed him, hugged him strong, and slapped him hard on his back. My little brother has grown up to be such a strong and wonderful husband and father. I am so proud of him. Almighty God would use his presence over the next several days in such a way that nothing would be the same if it were not for him being here.

To arrive in Tulsa before or at noon from the northeast means that you had to take a 6:00 a.m. flight, meaning that you had to be at the airport by 4:00 a.m. to be on time. Knowing this, it was time for the travelers to eat and relax. We headed to a local restaurant. Once we were seated and ordered some drinks, the children left the table to freshen up. This left Jim and I alone at the table.

At that time, Jim asked me, "How serious is this with Bert?" Prior to this, I had not been able or was not going to share the doctor's opinion to anyone, but Jim was different and he could handle it.

I said, "I have not shared this with anyone and will not, but I can tell you that the doctor shared with me yesterday that he has recently lost his father to COVID and that he does not see a path to recovery for Bert. That is why I started making phone calls."

My brother, in serious matters, is a man of very few words, and you always know his position.

"I understand," Jim said.

"Thank you for letting me unload this burden. It's better now that I have told you," I said. I never did tell anyone else. Sharing with my brother was sufficient. At this time, everyone came back to the table and we enjoyed lunch together.

We discussed who wanted to go and visit with Bert. Kelly, Josh, and I agreed on going and Coleen and Molly decided that they would wait to hear how Bert was doing.

We visited with Bert and she was rebounding from such a terrible day on Wednesday. As always, we talked to Bert, shared that Coleen, Molly, and Jim were in, and prayed for her, shared our love and everyone's love for her. Then we said our good-byes.

On the way out, the young nurse who was with Bert on Wednesday noticed us and came to talk with us. She shared that she was not with Bert as she had received other patients. She let us know the nurses and doctors in the COVID ward were talking and excited about Bert's progress and moving out of the COVID ward to another ICU ward.

This conversation gave us all a renewed sense of hope and we could not wait to share with everyone. The news of Bert's progress was received with joy and I updated family and friends via the group text message that I had been using.

After dinner, Molly went over to Megan's house, who lived about ten minutes away from our house. Kelly was at home, about fifteen minutes away from our house in a different direction. Coleen, Josh, Jim, and I were at home. Coleen went to lay down as it had been a long day.

Earlier in the evening, I had called the hospital and talked to Bert's nurse to find out how the move went. The move went without any issues and Bert was stable and all markers were the same. She was doing good. I shared that report with everyone and sent out the text message to family and friends.

Jim, Josh, and I stayed up and were talking in the kitchen when my phone rang at around 10:20 p.m. I saw that the call was from the hospital and I went into the front room and answered.

"Is this John Dunbar?" the voice asked.

"Yes."

They shared that Bert had gone into full cardiac arrest.

"I am only ten minutes away. I will be right there," I said. "How do I find her?"

"Come to the front desk and they will let you know."

As soon as I hung up I and yelled two words to my brother: "Cardiac arrest!" Then I yelled to Josh, "Josh, if you are coming, get dressed!"

I ran down the hall, changed my shirt, and put on some shoes. I ran to the front door and there was Josh waiting for me. We sped to the hospital and ran through it until we reached her room.

I was just ahead of Josh and I could see that the team was attempting heart resuscitation. I turned and hugged Josh and turned him away from the scene in the room. Right or wrong, I did not want him to see what was happening.

I was holding Josh when the doctor came out and shared that they had been working to restart Bert's heart. They had had some positive response, but it did not last. He shared that they could continue if we wanted. I asked them to continue. In addition, I asked the doctor, "Would you tell Roberta that Josh and John are here?" He said he would.

We were just down the hall from Bert's room and I was facing the room and could see the activity. I kept Josh in my arms. He could not see in the room at this time. After what seemed a long period of time, the doctor came out of the room and was walking toward us.

If you have been in a situation like this before, you know the look on the doctor or nurse's face. The doctor shared that there is no positive response at this time.

"We could continue, if you want," he said.

"Please stop," I said.

He nodded and walked back to the room.

It was 11:00 p.m. Central time.

I did not let go of Josh. Through my tears, I could barely speak. I said, "Josh, I have to let her go... I have to let her go!"

Josh held me up, and I do mean that he physically held me up. I could not believe what was happening. I was in shock. I never thought for a moment that she would not get off of the ventilator and be back with us.

The team started to complete their work and put up their equipment. As they walked past us, they shared their condolences. After the team had completed their work, Josh and I were allowed to visit with Bert. At this time, I called Kelly to let her know of Bert's passing. Kelly said that she was coming right over.

"I will go and meet her," Josh said. The nurse asked if Josh wanted him to go with him and Josh agreed.

I called our house and Megan answered the phone. I shared that mom was gone to be with the Lord.

"Are you sure?" she asked.

"Yes," I confirmed. "We are with her now and Kelly is on her way to the hospital."

Megan's response now was heartbreaking as she was in so much pain. The next voice on the phone was that of Coleen, but I did not recognize her voice.

"Megan?" I asked.

"No, it's Coleen. Jimmy is taking care of Megan."

I found out later that Megan became so upset that Molly thought Megan was going to run through the glass French doors that opened to the backyard, but Jim was able to comfort and restrain her. Molly shared that there was no way that she or Coleen could have done what Jim did, as Megan is a very strong young lady. Additionally, I now understand that when Josh and I left for the hospital, Jim instructed Coleen to call Megan and Molly and have them come over there right now. Through all of this, Jim provided comfort, kindness, love, smiles, and laughter as only he could do. Jim knew exactly what to do in every situation and he did it.

I tried to call Bert's sister, Helen, and texted her with no response. It was now about midnight in Tulsa and 1:00 a.m. in Pennsylvania where Helen lived. I decided that I would call in the morning when Ronnie, Helen's husband, was up for work.

I now had some alone time with Bert. I realized that she was not there in her body, but I just held her hand and touched her face. Losing a parent is a terrible loss, but losing someone who you became an adult with is different. Bert went to be with the Lord five weeks short of our 48th wedding anniversary.

I was thinking so many thoughts and how quickly the last fifty years had gone by. In addition, the text she sent me on Saturday, February 27 was preparing me for this. My thoughts were then and are now, *She knew she was going home to be with the Lord and she was preparing me.*

I knew that Kelly and Josh were coming now. Kelly and Josh were so brave, so strong, and this situation was so hard to believe, from such a good report earlier today to now.

We stayed quite some time, talking, crying, holding on to each other. Then saying good-bye "for now" as we will be together again someday in Heaven.

Josh rode with Kelly from the hospital to our house. Jim met me outside when I arrived. We hugged and cried. Upon entering, all five children were sitting together in the room that Bert loved to sit in. We were all together for the first time in years.

SATURDAY, MARCH 20, 2021 (SEVENTH *COMFORT FROM HEAVEN*)

Annette is a very close, very special friend of Bert's. This is a message from Annette:

Dear John and Family, I am writing to you all to share what happened twenty minutes after Bert went home to be with Jesus. On Saturday, March 20 at 12:20 a.m. (EST), my time in Pennsylvania, I was awakened by these lyrics: "There is victory in the camp, at the sound of El Shaddai." There was such a knowing of victory for my Dear Heart (Annette often called Bert "Dear Heart"). I was rejoicing, singing, and thanking the Lord! I was so happy! Believing that Bert was healed and soon I would be able to talk to her again. At 7:00 a.m. my time, John texted me that Bert had gone home at 11:00 p.m. their time in Tulsa, Friday evening.

Bert truly was healed, but not in the way I had thought. Thinking through the lyrics that had awakened me, I believe that there was such shouting when Bert walked into Heaven that awakened me. Later that day, I looked up the word Shaddai and it means "the God of Heaven". Yes! He was shouting along with loved ones to have my dear friend home! Bert and I shared Jesus, laughter, tears, fears, prayers, and our hearts. We sent pictures of the grandchildren and gardens. George Eliot wrote: "Oh, the inexpressible comfort of feeling safe with a person, having neither to weigh thoughts nor measure words, but to pour them all out, just as they are, chaff and grain together, knowing that a faithful hand will take and shift them, keep what is worth keeping and then, with a breath of kindness blow the rest away." Was that not our Bert? I miss her.

In Christ's Love, Nettie xooox ("Nettie" is what Bert called Annette)

SATURDAY, MARCH 20, 2021 (EIGHTH *COMFORT FROM HEAVEN*)

I do not know that I slept, but just sat up in bed trying to deal with Bert being gone. I remember thinking that from 5:30-6:00 a.m. Tulsa time, I would call Helen, as I knew that Ronnie would be up at that time. I called and Ronnie did answer the phone. I shared with him about Bert's passing and apologized that he was the one who was going to have to let Helen know about Bert. As always, Ronnie was gracious and understanding. He let me know that Helen was sleeping and we agreed to talk later in the day.

Later that afternoon, I called again and Helen and I talked. Helen then shared this with me:

"John, when Ronnie came in to tell me that Bert went home to be with the Lord, I knew. I already knew. I had a dream and in that dream, Bert was walking with Jesus and my mom. I woke up from the dream about 4:00 a.m. and then went back to sleep. So, when Ronnie came in and said my name, I knew Bert had passed and I knew where she was and who she was with. I knew!"

An aside: The dream that Helen received is exactly what I am referring to as "*Comfort from Heaven*". These comforts take many forms, some as dreams, feelings, sensing, or even a recognition of what has been a significant influence in preparation for, or as comfort after the fact. This is what this book is about: recognizing and appreciating that we all can receive "*Comfort from Heaven*".

Helen and I ended our conversation with the agreement that the dream was from the Lord and that is exactly where Bert was, who she was with, and what they were doing!

This dream was indeed the eighth ***Comfort from Heaven*** in preparation for unwanted news that was to come.

Saturday, March 20, 2021 (Ninth *Comfort from Heaven*)

We agreed that we would all meet at Megan and Justin's house. As Molly and I were entering through the garage, Molly stopped and was crying. I put my arms around her, and she shared that she felt Bert/Mom saying to her, "It will be OK." We embraced for a few minutes and agreed that it would be OK!

The ninth *Comfort from Heaven* for reassurance and to move forward.

Sunday, March 21, 2021 (Tenth *Comfort from Heaven*)

Many years ago when Kelly was a little girl, Bert had a nickname for her: Brownie. We had not called Kelly by that name for at least twenty years. Kelly sensed she heard her mom say to her, "Brownie, this place is amazing." When Kelly shared this with me, she said, "No one has called me that in years. It was mom letting me know about Heaven!" We agreed and laughed.

The tenth *Comfort from Heaven* delivered in such a personal way.

Wednesday March 24, 2021 (Eleventh *Comfort from Heaven*)

Since Coleen, Molly, and Jim arrived, I had been sleeping in our master bedroom. In that bedroom, there is a favorite picture of Bert's hanging on the wall on the right side of the bed. It is a picture of a lion and a lamb. Bert and I always agreed that she was the lion and I the lamb. In this depiction, our understanding between us has always been that, in the terms of the things of God, Bert was fearless and fierce as a lion, and as the lamb, my role was to bring support, whatever and wherever it was needed.

This morning as I awakened, I was lying in bed and looking at the picture of the lion and the lamb. During the previous days since Friday night, sadness overtook me many times. At those times, I just wept for the loss of my closest friend, the most influential person in my life. As I have shared many times, Bert has brought eternal value to my life. What eternal value means is being raised in an Irish Catholic family. While I knew about Jesus, I did not know Him personally. Bert guided me to establish a relationship with Him.

In recent years, I referred to Bert as "my counselor". People close to me knew exactly who I was referring to. Bert was and still is (as I remember many of our conversations and her wisdom) my counselor, guiding me in personal and professional matters.

As I lay there, I was thinking and looking at the lion and, in my mind, I said, *I don't think I can cry anymore.* That is when I heard in a gentle and authoritative voice, "Don't shed a tear for me!" Bert delivered such a message in a gentle, but strong voice. I received this from Bert as comfort as I know that she is in Heaven with Jesus, the love of her life, and all those who she held so close to her heart.

Since that day, while wonderful memories now carry sadness with them and I often weep when remembering them, my heart is no longer heavy with the loss.

The eleventh *Comfort from Heaven* had accomplished its purpose.

Thursday, March 25, 2021 (Twelfth *Comfort from Heaven*)

Kelly was home and she had been trying not to cry in front of her children, Johnny, who is eight-years-old, and Brooke, who is three-years-old. However, this is not always possible.

Brooke found Kelly crying, and she said, "Mommy, we prayed for Grammy to get better, and she is better, she is in Heaven. Sometimes I am sad and sometimes I am happy." Brooke just walked away after that and went back to playing.

Kelly taking it all in as the twelfth *Comfort from Heaven*, delivered by a three-year-old. It has become apparent that the comfort received from Heaven does not "fix" or "cure" everything we are going through, but simply picks us up and we are able to go forward once again.

Thursday, March 25, 2021 (Thirteenth *Comfort from Heaven*)

Megan had entered a painting of hers in a local art show and everyone agreed that we all would go to the show and then stop for something to eat afterwards. This was not easy for any of us, but we discussed that Coleen and Jim would be leaving the next day, so we went.

As we were parking the cars across from the gallery, it was becoming emotionally harder to go now for the first time without Bert.

After the show, we decided that we would walk to a nearby restaurant. At that time, Kelly and Molly became upset to the point of not wanting to go, but to just go home. We decided that I would go with them while the rest of the family went to dinner. Molly and I said good-bye to Kelly as she headed home. Molly was staying at Meagan and Justin's home and we went there and sat on the couch together.

After some time of sitting together, Molly said, "I hear Mom laughing at me. In a good way, I mean. Mom is saying, 'I always told you this was real and that someday, you would be seeking Him.' I would tell mom, 'No, I won't.' I feel that Mom wants me to seek God and not her."

I said, "Yes, I agrec to seek God. I desperately want to hear her, but Mom is not God. And maybe that is why I can't hear her."

Molly and I shared this thirteenth ***Comfort from Heaven:*** one message meeting multiple needs.

Saturday, March 27, 2021 (Fourteenth *Comfort from Heaven*)

Kelly found herself in deep thought about the passing of her mom when Brooke came to her and said, "Mommy, when people die who we love so much, we have to give extra love to the people who are here."

Words of the fourteenth *Comfort of Heaven* delivered through the heart of a three-year-old!

Tuesday, March 30, 2021
(Fifteenth *Comfort from Heaven*)

At about 7:00 p.m., Brooke said to Kelly, "God is in Heaven to protect Grammy until we get there".

The fifteenth ***Comfort from Heaven*** declaring there is a Heaven, there is a God, Grammy is there, and we are going there to be with her.

Tuesday, March 30, 2021
(Sixteenth *Comfort from Heaven*)

Megan's dream about Bert and Lucy

I had a dream that I was texting with mom from Heaven. I asked her if she saw Lucy. Lucy is a little white dog that has been a part of Megan's family, loved very much. She said, "Of course! I like the little white thing." This meant the little white clay memorial piece that has Lucy's paw prints in it that I got from the vet the night Lucy passed away.

Lucy passed on March 11. This is significant to me because mom had not seen the piece in real life as she was on the ventilator since midday March 2. This was something that I was not thinking about or would ever think that mom would like. She was so particular about what she liked and didn't like. I felt that she was communicating to me that she was close and could see what we were going through by picking something seemingly small and random. I had just put the piece up in the foyer the day or two before the dream. Before then, I had left it in its box and was not thinking about it all.

Also in that dream, I was trying to show Molly the text message that mom was sending from Heaven, but it was like the screen was blurry from the connection. Meaning I was trying to let Molly know also that mom could see us and was with us, even though she is in her rightful place in Heaven.

The sixteenth ***Comfort from Heaven*** received as Megan knows that her mom is still a part of her life.

Friday, April 2, 2021 (Seventeenth *Comfort from Heaven*)

Megan's dream about the little girl with the dark hair

I had a dream I was with mom in Heaven. It did not look like what I thought it would. It was like a resort; tables and chairs around a pool and lots of people walking around who were there waiting on mom.

She showed me to a little room and said, "Look, I have this, too". I looked in the room and saw a little girl with long dark hair in a ponytail jumping on a bed. The room was a cute little girl's room with a twin bed and maybe another bed in the room for mom, visually showing me that mom and the little girl were together.

The little girl looked about seven years old. Kelly's child that she lost (miscarried early in her fist pregnancy) would be about seven years old. I did not know this until later. When I shared this dream with Kelly, she mentioned the age her child would have been and, while I had the number seven in my head, I did not say this to Kelly. Kelly also shared that her and her husband Rob felt the child they lost was a little girl. I never knew that either. This dream was a couple of days before Easter, and I shared this dream with Kelly on Easter Sunday.

Seventeenth **Comfort from Heaven**, knowledge shared in a dream that never was shared before. Now validated!

Friday, April 2, 2021
(Eighteenth *Comfort from Heaven*)

Friday started out to be a very busy day at work. We had a couple of team members on vacation and then another team member called out sick. We were very short staffed. It is not that everything went wrong, it is just that nothing went smoothly. The point here is that I was not thinking about anything else, but getting and keeping the machines running.

As I took a break, I started remembering Beaver Lake in Arkansas. There are cottages there and years ago, Bert and I would go there for a getaway. The cottages are only about two and a half hours away by car from our home. I was also remembering the times we took the kids with us.

I was beginning to think that I wanted to do something for our anniversary that was coming up in a week. April 23 was going to be our 48th wedding anniversary and I actually thought about going to Beaver Lake for it. Thinking about this, I "felt" very happy inside. I could not explain it other than just "feeling happy inside".

Today was four weeks since Bert went home to be with the Lord and I was wondering if I would hurt the kids' feelings by considering this. Later that day as I was talking to Kelly, I asked Kelly her opinion. She thought it was a nice idea as she remembered how beautiful it was there at Beaver Lake. She said, "Dad, if you really feel that you want to go, then go."

When I got off the phone, I started looking up cottages for the 23rd and 24th. To my surprise, there were no vacancies to be found. Then I came across the same cottages we used to stay at years ago, but the search was the same: no vacancies. I thought there must be something wrong, so I decided to call. During the conversation, I began to understand that since COVID began, the business at Beaver Lake had risen some 30 to 40 percent as people do not want to stay in hotels, they want cabins and the outdoors. When I asked about the 23rd and 24th, I was told the 23rd was booked, but they did have one cabin left for the 24th and 25th and it was the only two-bedroom cabin they had.

We continued our conversation and I shared that my wife had just passed away four weeks prior and our anniversary was the 23rd. In addition, we had visited before just the two of us and another time with our children and we stayed in a two-bedroom cottage.

"Then you stayed in this cottage as it is the only two-bedroom cabin we have ever had," the gentleman said. "The guest books are there in the cabin and they are twenty years old, so if you wrote in the guest book, you should be able to find it."

I now was beginning to have that "happy inside feeling" again. I reserved the cottage. Molly and her husband Jay went with me. Our stay was perfect and relaxing and the location in the mountains was exactly what Molly and I needed, remembering past times in the very same cottage. Additionally, we looked through the guest books and found some notes that Megan, Molly, and Josh wrote many years before.

The eighteenth *Comfort from Heaven* now received as a "happy" feeling deep within me, knowing that the decision was correct.

Friday, April 9, 2021

10:00 a.m.

Kelly, Megan, Molly, and I went to Floral Haven to see the facility and the chapel where we will have our memorial service for Bert here in Tulsa. It was very emotional for the girls and as we were leaving, we stepped outside the chapel and we just held each other and cried. Then Kelly shared that she knew inside that our family was going to, in her words, "soar"! We all received this word of encouragement.

THURSDAY, APRIL 15, 2021 (NINETEENTH *COMFORT FROM HEAVEN*)

10:30 a.m.

Meagan and Chris Raccuia are very dear friends of Bert and I. In fact, I was honored to marry them in a Christian Wedding Ceremony. At the rehearsal party, my favorite picture of Bert was taken. When their first child Emma Rose was about four months old, they were in Tulsa visiting from their home in South Carolina. They visited us at our home and spent the day with us.

Now, a little over a year later, Meagan tells this story. "While taking Emma Rose (seventeen months old at this time) up for her nap, on the way to her bedroom, we passed by a table where we have a photo taken at our wedding with Bert, John, Chris (my husband), and I. I believe this was the first time Emma noticed the picture on the table. She went up to the picture, grabbed it, lay it down on the floor, and then pointed directly to Bert.

"I first said, 'That's Mrs. Bert and you got to meet her when you were a tiny baby.' She kept pointing to Bert and saying 'this' (her word at the time to want to know what/who something/someone was). So, I said, 'She's pretty, isn't she? She was such a sweet and kind-hearted lady who loved God and is now in Heaven.' As I said that, I realized that I never talked to Emma about God, Heaven, or the Bible. I've prayed for her and said prayers with her, but never talked to her about faith. Even though she was only seventeen months, I told myself it is never too early to start. After telling her about Heaven, I decided I needed to talk to her more about it after that. I truly think that there was a reason for this. Bert was always so strong in her faith and it was as if she was trying to help me talk to Emma about it, just as she did when she was with us."

I thanked Meagan for sharing this story with me. When I shared this with our family, I said, "Your mom's reach and her ability to influence continues!" This story brought **Comfort from Heaven** to us all as we remember Bert's love for children and her desire to teach.

Wednesday, April 21, 2021
(Twentieth *Comfort from Heaven*)

Kelly was shopping at a local store when she thought she saw Bert. This was heartbreaking and Kelly had a hard time keeping it together until she got home. As soon as Kelly pulled her car into the garage, she was overcome with sadness. Then Kelly felt that Bert was letting her know that she was with her dad and she was able to receive love from him. Bert was one of seven children with three older and three younger siblings. Being able to have time with her mom and dad was not always possible, but was very much desired by Bert.

This twentieth *Comfort from Heaven* was received as knowing that Bert was spending time with her dad who she loved so much.

Thursday May 20, 2021 (Twenty-first *Comfort from Heaven*)

Megan receives comfort in a picture of a garden, from Molly

I was sitting on her back porch looking out into the yard thinking/praying for God to just show me something that He is with us in this and that mom is okay, as I always do. What came to my mind was that the sign or comfort would come from one we would not expect. Right then, I received a message from Molly showing me a picture that reminded us both of mom. The picture was of a little wooden house in a garden surrounded by flowers. Molly said that she loved the picture and the words with the picture. What Molly thought was an inscription that went with the picture were actually the words of the song that means so much to me. They are the words from the song "There was Jesus," a song I know and that I know dad listens to and listened to throughout the time mom was in the hospital. I said to Molly that it was a song sung by Dolly Parton (one of our favorite singers) and let her know how much dad loves and listens to the song.

Twenty-first *Comfort from Heaven*, comforting to Megan that her sister Molly 1,200 miles away was in step with her feelings and emotions. Nothing separates us from the love of Christ!

Wednesday May 26, 2021

Nine and a half weeks since Bert went to be with the Lord

Megan and I went out to sit and talk. Moreover, as we were talking, Megan shared how much she misses her mom, knowing she is in Heaven and the fact that she can see us. Megan said, "I just wish I could talk to her. If I could just have a sign or an answer."

Thursday May 27, 2021 (Twenty-second *Comfort from Heaven*)

Megan's dream the next night after we talked

I was outside of mom and dad's house in the driveway and the car pulled up and it was supposed to be Josh and dad, but I could clearly see mom in the passenger seat. I opened the car door and said, "Mom is here!" Josh and dad could not see her, but I started talking to her. It was as if she knew how sad we were, but said, "I don't care." Not in a mean way, but in her way.

"You mean you do not want to come back?!" I asked.

She shook her head.

I asked, "Is it beautiful there?"

She said, "Yes, it is beautiful."

"Are you OK up there?"

"Yes."

Somehow, we got to talking about food. She said in Heaven, if you want food, it's like if you have a memory of a time you had something so good and you want it again, you can have exactly that. She said that is why you have those earthly experiences so that when you go to Heaven, you are given exactly what you want.

Another part of the dream, dad said, "Look what Gail is doing," and he showed me a video with a view from above a gravesite. One was mom's and one was Gail's future gravesite next to mom's (Gail is a lifelong friend of mom's and they always had great fun together and loved one another). This was just showing me their close friendship. Gail had drawn in the dirt with her hand a crown and a heart. They looked similar to the wooden statues that mom has a lot of. Kind of simple figures, but so sweet and can show much emotion. The names above them said "Bill" and "Billy". I do not know why, but it was definitely mom and Gail. Just showing the funny sense of humor they had together. This made me laugh and think of my own friendship with Jessi (my closest friend outside of family).

I shared this dream with Gail on Friday, May 28. She said, "Megan, these are the Lord's comforting words to you and me. I've been spending time in Hanover Township working on my family gravesites. It was a beautiful three days. When I was working the soil with my hands, I always remembered your mom's mom, Aggie, telling me how beautiful Bert's flowers always were, and she said Bert worked the soil well with her hands.

Twenty-second *Comfort from Heaven*, the activity in the dream validated by Gail who lives 1,244 miles away in Pennsylvania.

Tuesday June 22, 2021 (Twenty-third *Comfort from Heaven*)

FYI: I documented this as soon as I had time at the airport, just hours after I experienced it.

Father's Day weekend. I had the opportunity to spend this weekend with Molly and Jay at Jay's mom's home in Babylon, New York. The home is absolutely beautiful and being with Jay's family is always nice as they are so kind and thoughtful.

Driving to the airport, I received a call from Megan. Megan shared that she had been offered and accepted the position she had applied for. This is a position Megan has always wanted. It was at a local school for an art teacher in the 5th grade. This is same school system Megan and Molly graduated from.

As she was sharing the particulars about the position she had accepted, the compensation, benefits, and schedule all sounded so good! I was so happy and proud of Megan for this accomplishment. Then Megan shared that she was asked if she was familiar with art therapy and would she be able to facilitate art therapy sessions. As soon as she said the words "art therapy," something came over me and I could not stop crying tears of joy.

"I am losing it," I said. "It is the art therapy, and I cannot stop crying."

So many thoughts flew through my mind. Of course, Megan can facilitate art therapy; her mom was an excellent counselor and her older sister practices art therapy professionally.

Megan then shared that she is constantly praying for guidance to do the right thing and make the right decision. In addition, looking for confirmation in the small and normal things of life. She shared that the person interviewing her said that the school had been looking for a long time to hire a teacher that could lead art therapy, but until now, they had not found one. In addition, the person who was interviewing Megan was named Molly. The same name as Megan's twin sister.

"Megan, I am so proud of you," I said again.

Megan said, "I think mom would be proud of me."

"She is!" I said. Then in my mind's eye, I saw Bert and she was giving fist pumps with her right hand high into the air, throwing her whole self into it. She was repeatedly yelling, "Go, Tig, go! Go, Tig, go!" (Bert's name for Megan). She was not the mom of recent years, but she was young and strong and her hair was the natural color that I loved. Bert had the biggest smile on her face!

I told Megan, "Mom is rejoicing with you! She is so excited knowing what you are going to accomplish and the young people you are going to help."

We talked for a little while longer and said good-bye. Megan shared that she was happy for me that I saw and heard Mom.

Not since March 24 when I head Bert say to me, "Don't shed a tear for me," have I had any experiences of *Comfort from Heaven*. Today, in my mind's eye, I saw and heard Bert rejoicing, cheering, and participating in Megan's announcement! Seeing Bert so young, strong, and happy was not something that I had thought of, but it is so special to me, and, of course, Megan. Truly a *Comfort from Heaven*.

An aside: Since Tuesday when I experienced this ***Comfort from Heaven***, I have tried multiple time to visualize Bert like I saw her. I cannot, and the only thing I can think is this: If I can't visualize her now, then I did not visualize her on my own on Tuesday. Since this experience, I am at a different level of peace and comfort than before.

ACKNOWLEDGEMENTS

Summary "For Now"

What is shared in this book is what has touched our hearts, ***Comfort from Heaven*** as we call it. Given to our family as we mourn the passing of a friend, sister, wife, mom, gram, teacher, counselor, minister, and witness of the Love of God. The influence of the life Bert lived continues.

Understanding that what is contained in this book may be challenging or in conflict with teachings or training that you have had. This is understood completely. Again, the intent of this book is:

Acknowledge and honor Bert for her contribution to her family, friends, and many acquaintances

Encourage you, the reader, to seek Him with your whole heart and, as He has said, "He will be found".

A personal Savior He truly is, and your experience will be personal to you.

Thoughts, concerns, stories of your own, or prayer requests, contact

John H. Dunbar
thelionandthelamb228@gmail.com

CPSIA information can be obtained
at www.ICGtesting.com
Printed in the USA
BVHW062304011221
622875BV00006B/235